IMAGES
of Aviation

EDWARDS AIR FORCE BASE

This little cowboy is not afraid of the biggest plane on the Edwards ramp in the mid-1950s, the Convair YB-60. The boy might represent Boeing's B-52, which easily won a showdown with the Convair at the time for a contract as the U.S. Air Force's next heavy, long-range bomber. (Air Force Flight Test Center History Office.)

ON THE COVER: How many men can sit side-by-side on the wing of a Convair B-36? At least 85, with room to spare. The B-36 was built as an intercontinental strategic bomber, the first that was capable of carrying nuclear bombs inside the fuselage without any modifications. Not surprisingly, it was the largest production piston-engined aircraft ever built, with a wingspan of 230 feet. This image from the mid-1950s captures the camaraderie and glory of the flight line at the Air Force Flight Test Center, Edwards Air Force Base, where the immensity of the aircraft and operations perfectly fit the vastness of the Mojave Desert. (Air Force Flight Test Center History Office.)

IMAGES
of Aviation

EDWARDS AIR FORCE BASE

Ted Huetter and
Christian Gelzer

ARCADIA
PUBLISHING

Published by Arcadia Publishing
Charleston, South Carolina

Library of Congress Control Number: 2009942527

For all general information, please contact Arcadia Publishing:
Telephone 843-853-2070
Fax 843-853-0044
E-mail sales@arcadiapublishing.com
For customer service and orders:
Toll-Free 1-888-313-2665

Visit us on the Internet at www.arcadiapublishing.com

Pictured is a beautiful nighttime engine run of a Lockheed YF-104 using afterburner. Afterburn, what in Great Britain is called "re-heat," is the practice of dumping jet fuel into the engine exhaust behind the last set of turbine blades and igniting it. The additional combustion adds considerable thrust to the aircraft, but it also consumes fuel at an alarming rate, making the use of afterburner something pilots do cautiously. Versions of the exciting F-104 were used at Edwards as research aircraft and chase planes for decades, long after they left the U.S. military arsenal. (Air Force Flight Test Center History Office.)

CONTENTS

ACKNOWLEDGMENTS

We thank the Air Force Flight Test Center History Office (AFFTC) and the Photography Office at Edwards Air Force Base and the NASA Dryden Flight Research Center Photography Lab for their invaluable help and resources—in particular, Dr. Stephanie Smith of the Air Force Flight Test Center History Office, who patiently scanned so many images for us. We also thank Debbie Seracini at Arcadia Publishing, who made the first call to Ted to suggest doing a book about Edwards. If it were not for her patience, kindness, and inspiration, this project never would have happened.

All images used in this book come courtesy of the AFFTC and the NASA Dryden Flight Research Center (DFRC), unless otherwise noted.

INTRODUCTION

Sometimes the flight controllers at Edwards Air Force Base will allow airliners to fly through the base's usually restricted air space about 90 miles north of Los Angeles. The courtesy saves a few minutes of flight time for an air carrier descending into the Los Angeles basin. One would hardly think it's worth an announcement by the captain to the passengers, but more often than not, the pilot cannot resist expressing some delight, even reverential gratitude. "Ladies and gentlemen, we'll be arriving in Los Angeles a couple minutes sooner, because the good folks at Edwards Air Force Base have just allowed us to fly directly through their air space instead the usual jog around it. We'll soon be flying directly over Edwards's large, dry lakebeds. Now all that flat brown desert might not look too special from up here, but that's where the space shuttles first landed, and if you've heard of the expression 'the right stuff,' right down there is where it all started." If there are any pilots or aviation enthusiasts onboard, you can be sure they are craning their necks to catch a glimpse. Some might even let their imagination take flight and savor a moment being above Edwards, for the greatness that is Edwards Air Force Base extends from the ground to the edge of space.

Those dry lakes define the place we called Edwards. Situated on the southwestern edge of California's Mojave Desert at the lowest levels of the surrounding Antelope Valley, Rogers Dry Lake and Rosamond Dry Lake are souvenirs of wetter ancient times. Rogers is 44 square miles of hard, flat clay. Adjacently, Rosamond Dry Lake is about half that size. Edwards Air Force Base and its tenant facilities occupy land next to the playa, much like a California beach town hugs the coastline. Rogers's lakebed has been left undeveloped save for seven runways outlined with thick lines of tar. They point in all directions, the longest extending over 7 miles. It is the ideal place for aircraft that naturally land too fast, too long, or too unpredictably for conventional runways—like the radical, experimental flying machines that have been flown at Edwards since the early 1940s.

Before it was known as Edwards, it was Muroc—the reverse spelling of Corum. The Corum family established a little community on the edge of Rogers Dry Lake—then called Rodriguez Lake—early in the 1900s. The postal service did not want them to name the town Corum, because there was already service in a place called Coram. So despite some objections from the railroad because of another town with a similar name, they called it Muroc. The name stuck for decades.

In 1933, the military established a camp opposite Muroc along the southeast side of Rogers. It was on the edge of a vast expanse of desolate federal lands that were considered perfect for gunnery and bombing practice for the soldiers and airmen of the U.S. Army Air Force's March Field, located about 60 miles away in Riverside. In the summer of 1942, the tents there gave way to permanent structures for the establishment of Muroc Army Air Base. With World War II underway in the Pacific, the base became a flight training facility. By the fall of 1942, the Material Center Flight Test Site was established at the northern end of Rogers, laying the groundwork for what was to become the bread and butter of the lakebed airfield—flight-testing the most advanced planes in the business. It started with America's first jet aircraft, the Bell XP-59A Airacomet.

More name changes came as the two sites got busier. By the end of 1943, the so-called South Base became Muroc Army Air Field. A few months later, the North Base became Muroc Flight Test Base. Early in 1948, the army air field became Muroc Air Force Base—the U.S. Air Force was established the previous year. Finally, in June 1949, in honor of Capt. Glen W. Edwards, a test pilot at Muroc who died in a crash of the Northrop YB-49 Flying Wing, the facility was renamed Edwards Air Force Base.

If there is one Edwards project that will forever resonate with the general public and aviation folklore, it is the X-1 program. Originally called the XS-1 (Experimental Supersonic Contract No. 1), this Bell aircraft was the U.S. Air Force and National Advisory Committee for Aeronautics (NACA) entry in the race to break the sound barrier, shortly after the Second World War. While the program didn't exactly start it all, as flight test programs at Muroc were well underway by the time the first X-1 arrived in 1946, the X-1 program represented a geographical shift of major flight tests from the NACA's Memorial Aeronautical Laboratory at Langley Field in Hampton, Virginia, and the U.S. Air Force's Wright Field in Dayton, Ohio.

The first flights of the X-1 were scheduled for the winter of 1945 using Bell Aircraft flight crews to begin fulfilling the company's contractual commitments for the aircraft. Winter weather at Langley and Wright were not suitable for an aggressive flight program, and the season is the only time of year that rains typically flood the Muroc lakebeds, so Muroc was passed over as well; thus flights began at the U.S. Air Force's Pinecastle Field at Orlando, Florida. A modified Boeing B-29 bomber was used as a mother ship to air-launch the rocket plane. X-1 glide flights proceeded through the spring, but it became obvious to all parties that the supersonic program needed the clear skies and sparsely populated landscapes offered at Muroc. The torch was passed from the well-established, well-equipped, and more comfortable environs at Wright, Langley, and Pinecastle to the hardscrabble facilities at Muroc. By the fall of 1946, a small group of engineers and technicians from Langley formed the basis of what became a permanent NACA (and later NASA) presence at Edwards. It was also the beginning of an enduring and sometimes contentious partnership between the NACA/NASA flight research teams and the U.S. Air Force. On October 14, 1947, air force pilot Capt. Chuck Yeager flew the XS-1 past the speed of sound. The sound barrier became a myth, and it was not long before the desert air base became legendary.

In 1947, the NACA desert operation became the NACA Muroc Flight Test Unit. In 1949, it was the NACA High-Speed Research Station, then the NACA High-Speed Flight Station in 1954, and in 1959, became the NASA Flight Research Center—the National Aeronautics and Space Administration replaced the NACA in 1958. In 1976, it became the NASA Hugh L. Dryden Flight Research Center, and then in 1981, operations consolidated with NASA's Ames Research Center at Moffet Field, California, becoming the NASA Ames-Dryden Flight Research Facility. Finally, in 1994, it resumed its autonomy as the NASA Hugh L. Dryden Flight Research Center. Edwards has remained Edwards since 1949. The type of flying established there in the early 1940s became the business of the Air Force Flight Test Center at Edwards Air Force Base in 1951. Throughout the years, the Edwards family has included virtually all of the top corporate names in the aviation and aerospace businesses, a list that will evolve through the photograph captions in this book. Suffice it to say that Dryden and the Flight Test Center are the major players in the Edwards story.

Climate and landscape have been a part of the Edwards experience since the beginning. The Muroc years were truly harsh. Housing was scarce for civilians, who had to live in the small towns somewhat near the base. Base accommodations were primitive. Los Angeles was only 90 miles away, but it might as well have been 1,000. L.A. was another world—Hollywood, the big city, the beach, and the comfy corporate headquarters for many of the top aviation companies. Edwards's isolation could be intimidating to those who lived and worked there, but it also promoted kinship and a rugged, individual spirit centered not on the ranching and wildcatting tradition of the American West but on the new frontier of high-risk aerospace exploration. It is a spirit that did not diminish as the base grew in size and sophistication. The climate is still severe, and the landscape remains wild.

The photographs in this book are little windows into the first 40 years of flight at Edwards. Yet this peek into the past is sometimes so futuristic that it is a look outside the window today. Breaking the sound barrier became a metaphor for all activity at the desert outpost, both on the ground and in the skies. Engineers continued to push the limits of flight with bold new designs. Instrumented aircraft collected ever more data that was used to influence the designs of ever more future military and civil aircraft. In-flight testing of prototypes refined new flight vehicles and made sure the military was getting what it bargained for.

The desert air has been home to rocket planes and pedal planes, things that hover and fly backwards, planes with wings of all sizes and shapes, and planes that are even all-wing. The people associated with the flight projects at Edwards have always been tops in their fields. And despite the harsh climate, isolation, and demanding work, service at Edwards became a desired right of passage for anyone who wanted to be a part of the grandest story in modern aviation.

The U.S. Air Force claims that more first flights and record flights have been made at Edwards than at anyplace else. There have been a few last flights as well. All contribute to its legacy and greatness. If ever you find yourself in the skies above Edwards, remember those who came before you.

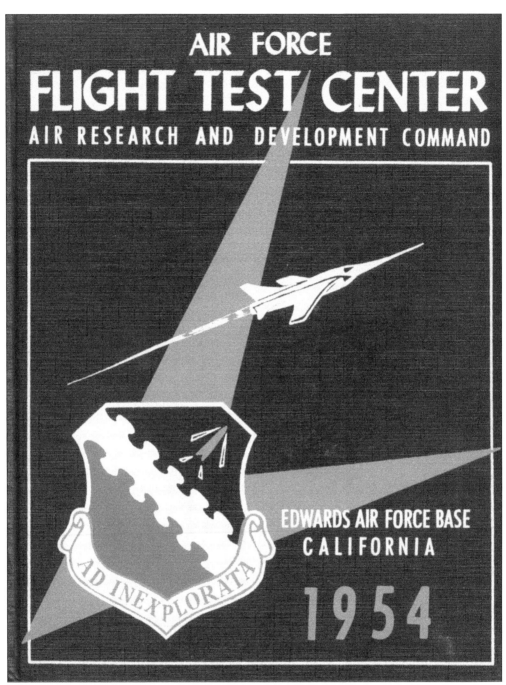

The Edwards yearbook was an informal publication with about 150 pages profiling the military and civilian activities at the base, complete with hundreds of smiling headshots of the people who worked there. Seen here are the shield and the motto of the Air Force Flight Test Center, *Ad Inexplorata* (Toward the Unexplored), from the 1954 yearbook. (Ted Huetter collection.)

One

FROM BOMBING RANGE TO SONIC BOOMS

This tower, located on the near Rogers Dry Lake some time before World War II, shows how basic the working conditions were in the beginning: tents, canvas shacks, trucked-in water, and a lot of sand. The view from this tower overlooking the flat lakebed must have been expansive (and the elevation probably provided a little relief from the hot, dusty ground). (AFFTC.)

Located on the eastern shore of Rogers Dry Lake, East Camp was a temporary base for units from March Field. Once World War II began, bombers—light and heavy—visited the site. The MUROC compass rose is visible in the top photograph with faint radials emanating from the center circle. Rows of tents are grouped on the top right of the aerial photograph, with the long lines of parked aircraft to the left, as seen more closely in the bottom photograph. Boeing P-26 Peashooter fighters and Martin B-12 bombers are clearly visible. Conditions were inhospitable at best, with temperatures of 120 degrees in the summer, snakes, almost constant windblown sand, and no escape from any of the three. Winter meant rain that accumulated on the lakebed, which caused the only landing surface on the site to become unusable until it dried out enough to support heavy aircraft again. (AFFTC.)

The Martin B-12s in both photographs are from the 1930s. The planes were based out of March Field, about 70 miles south of Muroc. During World War II, aircraft were sent to the dry lakebed to practice bombing, using bomb casings filled with concrete. (AFFTC.)

Looking more like setting up camp in a remote, arid war zone, the South Base Barracks made for primitive life in the early days of Muroc. (AFFTC.)

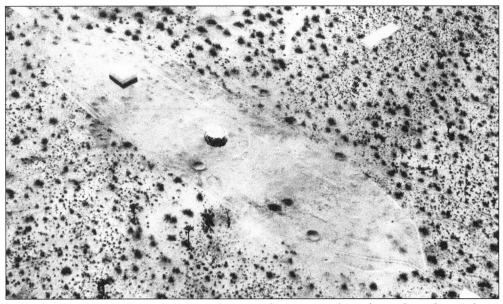

In the scrubby Mojave Desert, scraping the natural vegetation from the surface of ground was about all that was needed to fashion a target to bomb. Here one can see the outline of a battleship cratered with a few directs hits. There were several such targets etched in the Mojave landscape at Muroc. (AFFTC.)

The airmen at East Camp had the periodic duty of shoveling up spent shell casings from aircraft doing strafing runs. The three men first swept the casings into rows, not unlike farmers tossing hay, making their collection easier. Water jugs in the cart attest to the heat they faced during their work. (AFFTC.)

A B-25 passes over the "Muroc Maru" in 1944. The full-scale replica of a Japanese heavy cruiser was constructed on the southern portion of Rogers Dry Lake, providing bombers with a realistic target to practice on. The Army Air Force hired local farmers to build the vessel, made largely from wood and chicken wire. The bombs were inert so that strikes did little real damage and could be easily repaired. (AFFTC.)

Leaving a B-25 behind them, a happy group of visiting South Africans fills a jeep in 1943. (AFFTC.)

Flight crew and others pose in front of a B-25 at Muroc in 1943. The man second from the left is U.S. Army Air Corps pilot Glen Edwards. Edwards flew 50 bombing missions during World War II and became a test pilot at Muroc in 1944. He died in a crash during a test flight of the Northrop XB-49 in 1948. The base was named for him in 1949. Edwards, Canadian by birth, was regarded as a skilled ballroom dancer. (AFFTC.)

16

The Douglas XB-42 Mixmaster light bomber was an interesting product of the changing times in aviation. It was originally powered only by twin liquid-cooled piston engines turning two contra-rotating pusher props in 1943 (top photograph, with crew). When the U.S. Air Force cancelled that program, the plane was used to test Westinghouse turbojets that were fitted on each wing, making it known as the B-42A, pictured below. In 1946, Douglas developed the XB-42 into the exclusively jet-powered YB-43, becoming the first light jet bomber in the United States. Only two were built, as there were no production orders, but one continued to be utilized by the Flight Test Center as a jet engine test bed until 1953. The side-by-side, individual pilot canopies were unique features of the planes. (AFFTC.)

F3 ·820   2·28·4
CONSOLIDATED VULTE
MODEL XB32 NO. 41·142
LEFT NACELLE TURRET.

Three Consolidated XB-32 Dominator prototype long-range bombers were delivered to the U.S. Air Force between 1942 and 1943. With twin tails and long wings, the Dominators superficially seemed like a blimped B-24, but with Cyclone engines and other refinements, they were quite a different aircraft. One unique feature was the experimental machine gun turret meant to be remotely controlled. The turret was mounted under the engine nacelle, as seen in this photograph of the No. 2 aircraft, complete with the original U.S. Air Force identification sticker. The first Dominator was destroyed in a crash after 30 flights. The third plane, along with subsequent B-32 production aircraft, was modified with single fins. A few saw combat duty before the end of World War II, but production was halted in October 1945. Unfinished bombers were scrapped, and the last of the Dominator prototypes followed the same fate in 1949. (AFFTC.)

A Lockheed P-80 makes a high pass over what remains of the Muroc Maru. The 650-foot-long mock Japanese heavy cruiser was abandoned after the war for a while until it was removed altogether. Its "moorings" are almost impossible to spot today. (AFFTC.)

This is an aerial view of Muroc Field taken in 1946. The main runway has an overrun that extends out onto the lakebed with markings. The large hangars are visible along the flight line, as is a growing collection of smaller structures behind them. Those structures were soon contracted by aircraft manufacturers, who set up on-site shops to support their efforts at the base. (AFFTC.)

Looking like two sprouts in the garden of supersonic flight, this June 1947 photograph shows Bell Aircraft XS-1 Nos. 1 and 2 sitting in their loading pits at South Base with their B-29 mother ship behind them. Called XS for Experimental Supersonic, two years had passed since Bell was awarded the contract to develop and fly the world's first supersonic aircraft, but the project was moving too slow for the Air Material Command. That summer, the No. 1 plane, seen in the foreground, was used in an accelerated flight test program by U.S. Air Force test pilots. The No. 2 aircraft was used by the NACA. (AFFTC.)

Of the 125 air force test pilots in the Flight Test Division, Capt. Charles "Chuck" Yeager (left) was chosen as the lead pilot in the XS-1 program the summer of 1947. Here he is talking to air force chief of staff Maj. Gen. Henry H. "Hap" Arnold. On October 14, 1947, Yeager became the first person to break the sound barrier. (AFFTC.)

The top photograph shows X-1 No. 2 in the test fixture, perhaps waiting for an engine run. Its wings and horizontal stabilizers are off, its landing gear is partially deployed, and access panels are off. It was originally painted orange on the assumption that the color would make the plane more visible in the sky. It wasn't long before people on the ground realized it was too easily lost instead; accordingly, the X-1 and subsequent research planes were painted white (as seen in the photograph below). This aircraft became the NACA's to fly by mid-1947, as the U.S. Army Air Forces swept ahead in its pursuit of Mach while the NACA methodically advanced its speed with incremental gains, reviewing the data from each flight before venturing to the next mark. It took the agency another six months to reach Mach 1. The use of the "XS" moniker eventually became academic, with the "S" generally dropped in usage. Further references to the planes in this book will be in keeping with this practice. (Above: AFFTC; Below: DFRC.)

Skystreak crew members strike a proud pose with their Douglas D-558-1. Maybe it was a particularly hot day, as nobody else can be seen outside under these clear skies. Its main contribution to NACA flight research was in the pioneering use of vortex generators on the wings to improve controllability at higher speeds. The little streamlined rectangles fixed to a wing's upper surface soon became a common sight on jet bombers and airliners. (DFRC.)

NACA pilot Robert Champine gets some helping hands from the ground crew after a flight in a Douglas D-558-1 Skystreak. Champine arrived at Edwards in 1948 and made his first flight in the NACA X-1. Champine was hired as a replacement for Howard Lilly, who became the NACA's first pilot fatality while at the controls of another Skystreak in May 1948. Lilly's plane suffered catastrophic engine failure that led to a breakup of the fuselage shortly after takeoff. (DFRC.)

In October 1948, the base hosted the Society of Automotive Engineers and exhibited aircraft for the attendees. In the front row, from left to right, are: the McDonnell XF-85 Goblin, an experimental parasite fighter; a Bell X-1; a Convair XB-46; a McDonnell XF-88 Voodoo; and a Northrop YB-49 Flying Wing. Not a single one of the experimental aircraft on display went into production, although the XF-88 was reworked and accepted as the F-101 Voodoo. The X-1 was never intended to be anything but an experimental aircraft, of course. (AFFTC.)

Designed by giant road machinery maker R. G. LeTourneau, the Tournalayer was intended to solve the post-war housing problem. His enormous machines held internal and external wall framing into which the concrete was poured. After it cured for 24 hours, the machine picked up the house and carried it to the designated home site, lowered the new home to the ground, drew back the interior and exterior walls, and lifted the walls off, leaving the house standing by itself. It then drove away to start the process all over again. With so much open space, Edwards was an ideal spot to try this system. Over 100 such houses were built there between 1947 and 1949. (Both: AFFTC.)

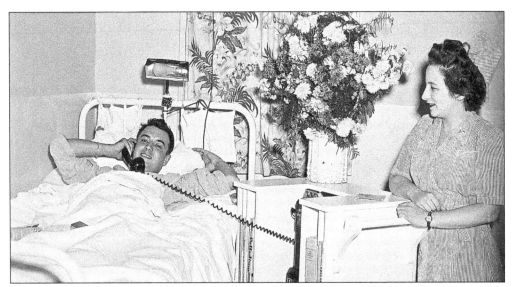

U.S. Army Air Force nurse Lt. Eugenie Novak watches T.Sgt. Edward Diltz use the new portable telephone from his bed at the base hospital in 1944. The phone rolled right up to the bed so that the patient could make calls without so much as moving a leg, which was considered quite an innovation in 1944. (AFFTC.)

It is thought that one day, computers will be almost human. In the 1940s at Edwards, they were human. These women, all with a math background and most with a college education, were hired as computers (that was their job title) to reduce raw data from filmstrips into numbers that could be graphed so that engineers could see what had actually happened on a given flight. Here women computers proudly pose in front of a snowman during an unusual winter in 1949. Enjoying desert snowfall at Edwards was a rare treat. (DFRC.)

Here is the sleek Convair XB-46 over the Antelope Valley near Edwards. The plane's maiden flight was on April 2, 1947, and it was delivered to the U.S. Air Force early the next year. Its straight wings and tail were clearly a holdover from the age of piston-powered medium bombers. Despite respectable performance, it was no match for Boeing's truly modern XB-47, which took to the skies in late 1947. Boeing was soon awarded a production contract with the air force, while only one of these beautiful Convairs was made. Pictured below is a dramatic B-47 takeoff boosted with 18 jet-assisted takeoff (JATO) rockets. (Both: AFFTC.)

With a maiden flight on May 9, 1949, the Republic XF-91 Thunderceptor was an unusual aircraft even for Edwards. It was designed as a short-range interceptor and in 1952 became the first combat aircraft to exceed Mach 1 in level flight. Many other features helped set the Thunderceptor apart from other aircraft: it had inverse-taper wings with pilot-controlled variable incidence; its takeoffs could be boosted with the assistance of twin built-in, liquid-fuel rockets over and under the turbojet tailpipe; and the main landing gear had wheels mounted in tandem. Two of the aircraft were built. This 1951 image shows one of them parked at South Base at Edwards. (DFRC.)

The venerable Boeing B-17 was an advanced design of the mid-1930s, shown above flying chase for the Northrop XB-35 in 1946 or 1947, but it seems antiquated compared to the modern lines of the first flying wing bomber on the drawing boards only six years later. Legendary aircraft designer John Northrop was dedicated to the development of the flying wing, a challenging configuration that takes aeronautical design to its most elegant essence. Northrop's first plane to research the concept took flight in 1929. He was awarded an army contract for the XB-35 bomber in 1941. While work began on the bomber, 10 different smaller, flying wings (such as the single-seat N-1M shown below) were test flown at Muroc during World War II. The first flight of the XB-35 was 1946. (Both: AFFTC.)

These aerial photographs of the XB-35 nicely show the airfoil's clean lines and camber. The teardrop blisters on the upper and lower surfaces of the wing were remote-control gun turrets. Two XB-35s were built at the Northrop plant in Hawthorne, California, and each had a wingspan of 172 feet. The pilots sat beneath the bubble canopy, while the bombardier's station was ahead of them on the leading edge of the nose. A third B-35 was designated the YB-35. (Both: AFFTC.)

These photographs give a sense of the scale of the XB-35, a truly large aircraft. It was powered by four Pratt-Whitney Wasp Major engines—two B-4360-17s and two B-R4360-21s—turning eight huge contra-rotating propellers. The contra-rotating props prevented torque problems. The engine nacelles added stability in the yaw axis. The bottom image shows several men pulling the props to move oil that has pooled at the bottom of the radial engine cylinders. They are standing on a platform that gives them access to the props and can be wheeled from one group of blades to the next. Powered up, they sounded like nothing else in the air. (Both: AFFTC.)

Here is a happy group after the first flight of the XB-35 on June 25, 1946. They are, from left to right, Northrop test pilot Max Stanley, flight engineer O. H. Douglas, Muroc Army Air Force Base commander Col. Signa Gilkey, and copilot Fred Bretcher. (AFFTC.)

One B-35 sits on the ramp while another performs an elegant bank overhead. (AFFTC.)

The B-35 program was cancelled soon after it started to convert the flying wings to all-jet powered YB-49s. The cleaned-up design was probably the most futuristic-looking flying machine on the flight line from 1947 to 1950. Two YB-49s were flown at Muroc. Although underpowered with eight J-35 jets, the YB-49 had a top speed of 520 miles per hour and was the longest-ranging jet at the time. This radical aircraft became forever associated with the desert air force base when pilot Capt. Glen Edwards and crew were killed on a test flight of the plane on June 5, 1948. The air base was named after Edwards in 1949. The remaining YB-49 was destroyed in a taxiing accident in 1950. (Both: AFFTC.)

One reconnaissance version of the YB-49, the YRB-49A, flew until 1952. The aircraft had provisions for photographic equipment in the center body, and in addition to four Allison J-35s in the wing, it carried two more J-35s in pods slung under the wing. The YRB-49 had better speed and range than the YB-49, but its handling was not superior to its sister ships, and eventually the U.S. Air Force ordered it and all the other Northrop flying wings to be scrapped. Northrop flying wings returned to Edwards 35 years later with the B-1 bomber. (Both: AFFTC.)

A Douglas D-558-2 is in a test stand during a rocket motor run in October 1949. While the D-558-1s were intended to explore the transonic realm, the -2 series was intended to linger in the supersonic realm. But unlike the X-1, the NACA intended it to be ground-launched. To do this, Douglas designed the airplane to have both a jet engine and a rocket motor. Visible just to the right of the stepladder on which the engineer is standing, almost at the fuselage's bottom, is the engine inlet for the Westinghouse J-34-40. It exhausted beneath the fuselage, under the U.S. Air Force insignia. Buried in the back of the fuselage was a Reaction Motors LR-8 four-chamber rocket motor meant to take over once the aircraft was at altitude for the experimental portion of the flight. The arrangement was less than successful, and the NACA returned the second airframe to Douglas to have its jet removed so it could be just an air-launched rocket plane. That plane, Tail No. 144, was the first to reach Mach 2 and hangs in the National Air and Space Museum in Washington, D.C. (AFFTC.)

Two Lockheed XF-90 airframes were built, one seen above in the engine test stand in 1949. The first U.S. Air Force jet with afterburner and a variable-incident vertical stabilizer, the aircraft lost out to the McDonnell XF-88 (which itself was rejected in favor of the F-101). The first aircraft was eventually shipped to the NACA Lewis facility at Cleveland, Ohio, where its robust airframe was tested to destruction. The second aircraft was sent to Frenchman Flat in the Nevada desert, where it was intentionally subjected to a series of atomic blasts to see what the effects would be. (AFFTC.)

Two

THOSE FABULOUS FIFTIES

This neatly arranged composition of Edwards's experimental aircraft reflects the promise and the determination of flight research at the beginning of the 1950s. As much as the first decade of flight saw a wide variety of aircraft shapes and configurations before the field settled on a few that worked best overall, the first decade of supersonic flight was an equally exciting time of daring designs, not without its share of missteps and tragedies. (DFRC.)

This is the entrance to the base through South Gate. It is not very remarkable for an air force base except that the two large chief hangars in the background show that the gate was quite close to the main facilities. Decades later, the gates were many miles from the core. The "swamp cooler" or evaporative cooler on top of the guard shack is an indication that this base in the southwest. (AFFTC.)

The South Base ramp is pictured on an undisclosed date, perhaps during an open house, when families, friends, and people from the surrounding communities were invited to visit the base and see some of the experimental aircraft whose booms and roars had been echoing across the desert. In the background is the control tower, which has been preserved and is on display near the West Gate entrance to the base. (AFFTC.)

Even by the year 2010, most of Edwards AFB and the immediate surrounding area look much like this, although the photograph was likely taken in the very early 1940s. In the distance stand the San Gabriel Mountains, the chain that separates the Mojave Desert from the Los Angeles basin. (AFFTC.)

Above is an aerial view of South Base in the late 1940s. In addition to the C-47s, there is a B-25 and the NACA's P2B-1S mother ship. In the lower right sits an F5D Skylancer, a P-80, and Douglas D-558-2. When the Main Base, located near the top of the picture, was built, the two large Quonset hut–like hangars on the flight line were actually towed a mile across the desert to the new facility, where they remain in use 60 years later. (AFFTC.)

Built for the U.S. Marines, the barracks above were made available to the growing NACA civilian population coming to work at the base (then still Muroc, but soon Edwards). Dubbed Kerosene Flats for the odor of the heating oil that permeated everything, they were cold in winter, hot in summer, and sand-filled most of the time. Their thin walls had sometimes been poked by the horns of free-ranging cattle that wandered the area (the solution for which was to hang a picture over the hole). Post-war housing demand was so high that little was available. Some engineers were happy to make do with converted chicken coops. The benefit of Kerosene Flats was that it was on base, offering a short walk to work. As seen in the photograph below, trailer parks adorned with lofty television antennas became another option for civilians in the 1950s. (Both: AFFTC.)

This is the instrumentation office at Edwards in the 1950s. Noteworthy are the wall paintings that show not just the advances in flight through history but also the latest aircraft the base engineers have worked on. What is striking is the coexistence of propeller aircraft with jet aircraft. This is also the era of slide rules and pencils, graph paper and French curves, as well as government-issue metal desks. (AFFTC.)

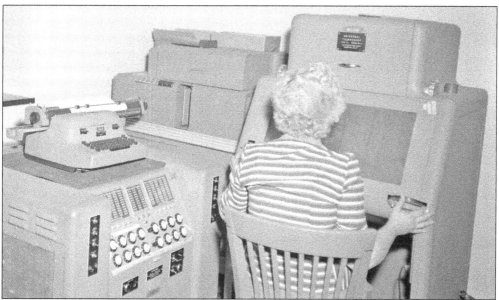

Unlike in years past, this computer sits at a modern light box to read film. Her right hand advances the film, and her left hand backs it up. This is a far cry from the early days at Muroc, when NACA computers did all the work by hand, right down to plotting graphs with French curves. (DFRC.)

Shortwave radio made it possible for those in the service to talk to distant friends and family. This sort of system allowed hometown ham radio operators to put families together via the airwaves. For example, the ham would agree to get an airman's relative to the radio the next week at 6:00 p.m. so the family members could talk at the arranged time on the radio for no cost. Long distance phone calls in those days were very expensive. (AFFTC.)

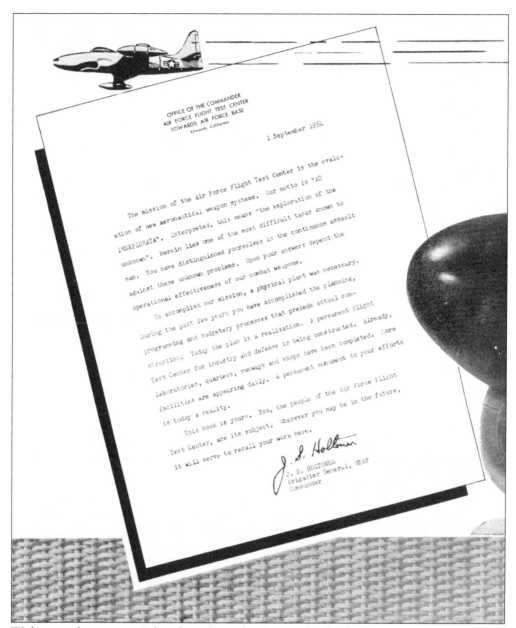

OFFICE OF THE COMMANDER
AIR FORCE FLIGHT TEST CENTER
EDWARDS AIR FORCE BASE
Edwards, California

1 September 1954

The mission of the Air Force Flight Test Center is the evaluation of new aeronautical weapon systems. Our motto is "AD INEXPLORATA". Interpreted, this means "the exploration of the unknown". Herein lies one of the most difficult tasks known to man. You have distinguished yourselves in the continuous assault against these unknown problems. Upon your answers depend the operational effectiveness of our combat weapons.

To accomplish our mission, a physical plant was necessary. During the past few years you have accomplished the planning, programming and budgetary processes that precede actual construction. Today the plan is a realization. A permanent Flight Test Center for industry and defense is being constructed. Already, laboratories, quarters, runways and shops have been completed. More facilities are appearing daily. A permanent monument to your efforts is today a reality.

This book is yours. You, the people of the Air Force Flight Test Center, are its subject. Wherever you may be in the future, it will serve to recall your work here.

J. S. Holtoner

J. S. HOLTONER
Brigadier General, USAF
Commander

With so much activity at Edwards in the mid-1950s, it is hard to believe that so much was done by so few. So few that nearly every individual's photograph is in a book about the same size—and look—of a city high school yearbook. This image is from one of the introductory pages in the 1954 Edwards yearbook; it is a letter written by the base commander, Brig. Gen. J. Stanley Holtoner. Holtoner flew 42 combat missions during World War II and assumed command of the Air Force Flight Test Center in 1952. The bulbous projection on the right side of the image is the nose of an F-86D. (Ted Huetter collection.)

USAF
EXPERIMENTAL FLIGHT
TEST PILOT SCHOOL

The Test Pilot School at Edwards makes use of its Pilot's long hours in conventional aircraft and jets. Applicants who should have a good engineering background and recent combat experience, are as thoroughly schooled in mathematics, engineering and aerodynamics as they are in the business of flying. The combination of these facts helps to produce the man the Air Force needs for the job. When they complete the six months' training, they become full partners in the air-ground technical teams which "road-test" every piece of equipment the Air Force buys.

School work area

This page in the test center's yearbook spells out what it takes to be a test pilot at Edwards. The school's roots date back to September 1944, when the Air Force Technical Service Command established the Flight Test Training Unit at Wright Field in Dayton, Ohio. The name was changed to the Air Material Command Experimental Test Pilots School in 1949, and the school, under a slightly different name, was moved to Edwards in February 1951. From the yearbook in 1954: "The primary mission of the AFFTC is to accomplish flight test of aircraft, power plants, components, and allied equipment, and research and development related to such tests; to plan for control and operate special test facilities for contractors and other government agencies, in support of the mission of the Air Research and Development Command." (Ted Huetter collection.)

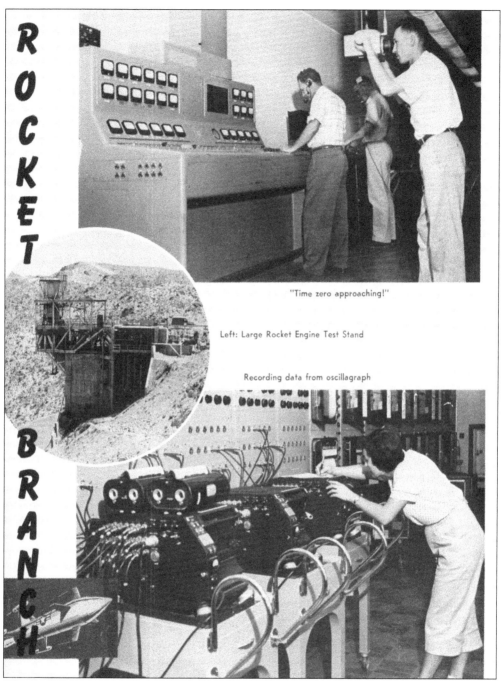

"Time zero approaching!"

Left: Large Rocket Engine Test Stand

Recording data from oscillagraph

There are some steep hills overlooking Rogers Dry Lake that were perfectly suited for rocket engine test stands. The site was far enough away from the main base to not interfere with flying operations, and rocket branch employees living at Edwards could commute to work via the "Rocket Test Bus." The hills literally spewed fire and smoke when the large rockets were lit. The rocket site was later used in support of the Apollo space program in the 1960s, rattling windows in the town of Boron, located about 10 miles away, just north of Edwards. This page from the yearbook gives a hint of the activities on the hill. (Ted Huetter collection.)

BASE SCENES

Tallest Tower

Downtown Edwards

Flight line formation

NCO Club

Edwards was not unlike many small towns in the Mojave Desert—from the street, they seem deserted, for more often than not, the weather is too hot, too cold, or too windy for a casual stroll, as illustrated in this page from the yearbook. (Ted Huetter collection.)

Here the Republic YF-96 is ready to be anchored to the thrust stand for an engine run. Manufacturers sent preproduction aircraft to Edwards to demonstrate that the aircraft met the U.S. Air Force's requirements before the model was accepted and put into production. (AFFTC.)

A Northrop F-89 Scorpion is being prepared for an engine run in February 1951 on a part of the ramp at South Base. The XP-89 first flew in 1948, and production was authorized in 1949, something that reflected both the chilling international environment and the rapidity of advances in aeronautical technology. While today it may take 20 years from model acceptance to delivery of a fighter, in the 1950s, a fighter model could be accepted and discarded within five years, sometimes even less. (AFFTC.)

While the B-29 mother ships helped usher in the age of supersonic flight, air tanker versions like the KB-29 helped nurse the new generation of jet bombers in the late 1940s and early 1950s. This 1952 photograph shows a KB-29 refueling a B-47 over the mountains bordering Antelope Valley near Edwards. Despite the B-36's 10,000-mile range, it was easy prey for jet fighters as a strategic bomber meant to strike the Soviet Union. The new B-47 had the speed but not the range—it had to be refueled in flight to satisfy the demands of the Strategic Air Command. In 1948, conversion of a number of B-29s from bombers to tankers began, using a new aerial refueling boom developed by Boeing. The boom allowed an operator, in what was formerly the tail turret, to "fly" the telescoping pipe to a thirsty aircraft below. It was a very practical system that quickly and effectively delivered fuel, resulting for the first time in a truly global reach for the nation's flying arsenal. (AFFTC.)

This is a wind tunnel model of the Martin XB-51 medium-range bomber. As with many other medium bombers of the late 1940s and early 1950s, placement of the jet engines remained a question. In this case, two of the engines were nestled next to the fuselage, while the third was buried in the aft section of the fuselage and had an air inlet on top of the fuselage, ahead of the vertical stabilizer. (AFFTC.)

The clean lines of the XB-51 are evident as the plane banks over Rogers Dry Lake, which here does not look particularly dry. There were two prototype XB-51s; however, both were ultimately destroyed in pilot-error crashes in 1952 and 1956. Martin lost the contract when the U.S. Air Force decided to buy the British Canberra instead but in turn won a contract to build the Canberra under license, producing it as the B-57A. (AFFTC.)

The XB-51 takes off from Edwards aided with JATO bottles. The term JATO, short for Jet Assisted Take Off, might seem a misnomer, since they were actually rockets, but the term stems from a period when "jet" covered the expansion of gases and their exhaust out a nozzle for propulsion, something that describes both rockets and jet engines. We still speak of a "jet" of steam. (AFFTC.)

The Martin XB-51 was temporarily cast as the Gilbert XF-120 in the 1956 film *Toward the Unknown*, starring William Holden. For its role, the aircraft had its actual name painted over and a new name and number applied. The film also featured the X-1 and X-2. (AFFTC.)

The B-50 was raised on jacks located at South Base so the X-1-3 could be rolled underneath to the mother ship's loading bay. The third X-1 was delivered to the NACA in 1951. Pilot Joseph Cannon made one glide flight in the plane in July of that year, then, following a captive flight with the B-50 in November, the aircraft was destroyed on the ground during an accidental explosion that also ruined the mother ship and injured Cannon. Notice that the X-1's cockpit door is open in the takeoff photograph. It will remain so until the pilot climbs in and closes it behind him at an altitude of about 25,000 feet. The pilot will ride a small, rickety elevator down a few feet from the bomb bay so he can climb into the experimental plane. A crew member handles the door, which the pilot latches. (Both: DFRC.)

This image shows the Bell X-1A over Rogers Dry Lake. Flying with it is a U.S. Air Force F-86 being used as a chase plane. Chase planes were and remain an integral part of flight research, providing the pilot of the experimental aircraft another set of eyes. Even though many X-planes flew at speeds faster than the chase plane could reach, the chases pilots were there to pick up the X-plane as it slowed and approached the base. (DFRC.)

The X-1A and X-1B reached Mach 2 by 1953. Chuck Yeager became the first Mach 2 U.S. Air Force pilot while flying the X-1A. On one flight, the plane went violently out of control at Mach 2.44 and 75,000 feet. Yeager regained control after dropping 50,000 feet and landed safely. This experience, and those of others in the X-1A and X-1B, showed that these designs had reached their dicey limits. It is clear in this image of the X-1B how carefully the equipment was packed into the aircraft, with virtually no space wasted. (DFRC.)

These two photographs are of the B-29 mother ship with the X-1A (below) and the X-1B with a proud crew (above). The nose art above leaves no doubt that this mother stork is carrying a Bell Aircraft baby. Below, the super-cooled rocket fuel oxidizers caused the skin of the research plane to develop a white coat of frost, clearly seen on the X-1A. The X-1A on the previous page still shows a little frosting as it glides back to Rogers Dry Lake, because it still carries a small amount of oxidizer. (Both: AFFTC.)

In the top photograph, crew members prepare for a flight with an X-1B in the bomb bay. Since there is no frost on the fuselage, it appears to be a captive-carry flight. Nevertheless, the X-1 pilot, who is being given his parachute, wears a partial pressure suit and helmet (the outer garment is merely a protective cover for the suit itself). The crew member about to emerge from under the P2B-1S carrying a helmet is likely the one who will attend the pilot as he climbs into the X-1. Both will wear oxygen masks in the bomb bay because of the altitude at which the activity will take place. Below, the mother ship with X-1B taxis toward the ramp that went to the lakebed from the Flight Research Center. (Both: DFRC.)

The first three generations of American fighter aces are represented in this photograph. On the left is Jack London, World War II ace; in the middle stands Fred Libby, World War I ace; and on the right is Iven Kincheloe, jet ace from the Korean War. Behind the three men are two widely separated eras of aircraft, a jet and a pre–World War I monoplane. (AFFTC.)

This pose, something done for other X-planes as well, was meant to show what was necessary to accomplish a research or test flight. It underscores the fact that it never was just one man wrestling a plane across an invisible boundary into the unknown. Iven Kincheloe stands at the bottom in front of the Bell X-2. Behind him are the ground support crew and engineers, the medical crew, the fire and rescue crew, the B-50 and launch crew, the chase crew and aircraft, the helicopter rescue crew, the loading crew, and the telemetry crew. (AFFTC.)

Air force pilot Iven Kincheloe stands next to Milburn "Mel" Apt, sitting in the cockpit of the X-2 rocket plane. The X-2 was Bell's swept-wing successor to its straight-wing X-1. The X-2 was designed to explore Mach 2 and Mach 3 flight and became the first aircraft to reach Mach 3. On September 27, 1956, Apt would set an unofficial world speed record of Mach 3.196 in the plane, only to be killed when the aircraft broke up due to inertial coupling. (AFFTC.)

Apt and Kincheloe playfully try to stuff the base commander into the cockpit of the X-2. Readily apparent from this angle is just how small cockpit was. This typified almost all the early high-speed research aircraft. (AFFTC.)

Iven Kincheloe talks to officers and
engineers following a flight in the X-2.
He hasn't even had time to get out of
the partial pressure suit, which is only
slightly undone around his shoulders
but has the gloves removed. Necessary
for anyone flying above Armstrong's
Line at about 63,000 feet, the suits were
very uncomfortable. After his X-2 flight
to almost 127,000 feet in September
1956, Kincheloe was considered the
"first of the spacemen." (AFFTC.)

Iven Kincheloe is holding curvy film star
Rita Moreno by her sash in the Officers
Club. Moreno had been awarded the
honor of Miss Sonic Boom, evidenced
by her form-fitting sash, much to the
pleasure of the officers. (AFFTC.)

The X-2 had a nose gear and two skids, and this landing left something to be desired, as the deep groove carved into the lakebed indicates. The first of two X-2s was destroyed in an explosion during a Bell Aircraft captive-carry flight in 1953. Flights at Edwards in the second plane began over a year later. (DFRC.)

The Bell X-2 has come to a stop on Rogers Dry Lake, and rescue vehicles are descending on the aircraft to extract the pilot and service the aircraft. The photograph was taken from the passenger seat of the second vehicle arriving on the scene. Roaring just overhead in a salute is an F-86 that flew chase for the X-2. (AFFTC.)

Pictured here is the wreckage of the ill-fated X-2 assembled in a hangar at the High-Speed Flight Station after Mel Apt's fatal crash. For two years, the X-2 was flown only by Pete Everest and Iven Kincheloe, until highly regarded test pilot Mel Apt was asked to take the plane past Mach 3—the first Mach 3 flight ever—on his inaugural flight in the plane. He made the mark but soon after heading back to the field the plane violently diverged. Out of control, he managed to separate the ejection capsule from the fuselage but was unable to bail out of the capsule before it crashed into the Edwards bombing range, 5 miles from where the rest of the aircraft impacted. (Both: DFRC.)

Boasting the behemoth Convair B-36 up front, the flight line at the Air Force Flight Test Center in the mid-1950s was an impressive sight. Behind the B-36 are Boeing bombers B-29, a new B-52, and a couple of B-47s, with nearly a dozen F-100 and F-86 fighters. The B-36 was built as an intercontinental strategic bomber, the first capable of carrying nuclear bombs inside the fuselage without any modifications. Not surprisingly, it was the largest production piston-engined aircraft ever built. (AFFTC.)

From this 1953 photograph, it is clear that the Convair YB-60 evolved from the Convair B-36. The YB-60 was intended to compete for the U.S. Air Force contract for a new long-range strategic jet bomber, and it lost to the more technologically advanced Boeing B-52. (AFFTC.)

An YB-60 rotates on takeoff from the Flight Test Center in January 1953. (AFFTC.)

This carefully posed photograph shows the men and material necessary to conduct a flight test program—in this case, a flight test of the Douglas D-558-2 Skyrocket. NACA pilot Scott Crossfield stands at the nose of the experimental aircraft, while six ground crew line up next to the cockpit. Behind the ground crew stands the man responsible for fueling the aircraft, along with some bottles of compressed gas. Two U.S. Air Force F-86 chase planes are next, with their pilots and ground crew next to them. The P2B-1S crew stands in front of the mother ship. Surrounding the aircraft and crew are ground support vehicles, including a fire truck. (DFRC.)

The photograph at left shows P2B-1S NACA pilots Neil Armstrong (left) and Stan Butchart (right) greeting an unidentified officer before a flight in the converted bomber. P2B-1S was the navy's designation for the Boeing B-29. The aircraft was used as the mother ship for the Douglas D-558-2 because the D-558 program was navy-sponsored—this explains the absence of an "X" designation for the aircraft, since it was the air force that gave that appellation. The mother ship was dubbed "Fertile Myrtle," a term for a mother of frequent pregnancies, an appropriate moniker for an airplane that dropped one airplane after another, as it were. Notice the Skyrockets stenciled on the plane next to the nose art. Each stencil denotes a carrier flight. (Both: DFRC.)

In 1956, Fertile Myrtle was carrying a D-558-2 on a mission when engine no. 4 began to run away. The crew of Stan Butchart and Neil Armstrong shut it down and feathered the propeller, but it unfeathered and began to spin again. They feathered it twice more, only to see it begin to spin up again each time. Now out of hydraulic reserve, the propeller began spinning uncontrollably. Jack McKay, hearing all this while in the D-558-2, asked to be dropped even though he wasn't ready for a flight, and they released him. Barely five seconds later, no. 4 engine's propeller blew, slinging its blades in four directions. Armstrong later said it "looked like the kitchen sink going by the cockpit" as the blades went in different directions. One blade passed through engine no. 3, killing it, then continued through the bomb bay where the D-558-2 had been moments before (and would very likely have killed McKay had he still been there), exited the other side of the fuselage, and passed through the bottom of engine no. 2's nacelle. The two pilots limped back to base on two engines while McKay successfully fended for himself. (DFRC.)

The P2B-1S sits on jack stands, hoisted into the air so that the D-558-2 can be dragged underneath and loaded into the bomb bay. There were two ways of loading the Skyrocket, since it did not fit into the X-1 pit. One was to raise the mother ship on jack stands, which was usually done in a hangar. The second was to raise the mother ship on a set of hydraulic jack pads embedded in the concrete ramp. The latter process was faster and easier, but was limited to periods when winds at Edwards were below 15 knots. This restriction severely limited the jack pad use. (DFRC.)

A beautiful duet with air force and navy partners: a trusty F-86 Sabre flies chase for the navy's Douglas D-558-2 Skyrocket. The first XF-86 was flown at Edwards on October 1, 1947. (DFRC.)

On November 20, 1953, NACA pilot Scott Crossfield became the first human to exceed Mach 2. The Douglas D-558-2 (Tail No. 144) was a pure rocket plane meant to explore the realm of transonic and supersonic flight. The only flight to Mach 2 came after several failures, followed by a carefully planned trajectory and a clean up of the airframe. NACA mechanics chilled the water-alcohol fuel mixture and cold-soaked the tanks in order to squeeze just a few gallons more of fuel, then waxed the airplane to make it more slippery. Crossfield is seen here talking to the news cameras about the record-setting flight. The close-up is Crossfield posing in the Skyrocket's cockpit. (Both: DFRC.)

Here Scott Crossfield is shown wearing an early full pressure suit, probably a David Clark Model 12 Navy for use in the D-558-2. What is seen is only the outer cover, meant to protect the material underneath. Beneath that are the layers that actually protect the pilot above Armstrong's Line. An emergency oxygen pack is on his back. (DFRC.)

This early 1954 photograph shows the three D-558-2s parked on the ramp with a B-50 mother ship. Only the one on the right is the pure rocket plane, as the other two have inlets for a jet engine below and beneath the cockpit. The telephone booth looks like it was meant to give a nervous pilot the last chance to call home before a flight, but was in fact just a guard shack. (DFRC.)

The X-3 Stiletto is being unloaded to the lakebed prior to a flight in 1956. Although the aircraft looked stunningly fast, it was underpowered and possessed some frightening handling characteristics, such as serious longitudinal instability called inertial coupling. The X-3 was expected to allow engineers to learn about aspects of Mach 2 flight, including heating from skin friction, so the plane was built with a unique structure involving titanium for the first time in the assembly of an aircraft. (DFRC.)

Air force test pilot Maj. Arthur "Kit" Murray poses in front of the Douglas X-3 Stiletto. The X-3 had the most unusual entry mode of any X-plane: the seat descended beneath the fuselage like an elevator, and once the pilot was seated, he and the seat rose back into the fuselage for flight. The ejection was downward. (AFFTC.)

A Northrop X-4 Bantam is shackled to the test fixture for an engine run in October 1949. The X-4 was the smallest of the first generation of X-planes. Two X-4s were built to investigate the unstable flight characteristics of semi-tailless aircraft (which had no horizontal stabilizer) near supersonic speeds, something experienced in World War II with the German Me 163 rocket plane. (AFFTC.)

Complete with aloha shirts, NACA technicians give the once-over to the No. 2 Northrop X-4, here seen in the all-white paint scheme favored by the NACA. The X-4 initially pitched, rolled, and yawed unfavorably at about Mach .88, but incrementally, modifications led to improvements at slightly higher speeds. Ultimately, the X-4 proved that transonic flight with a semi-tailless aircraft was not the best way to go. (DFRC.)

The design of the Bell X-5 came largely from the German Messerschmitt P.1101 of the Second World War. Both aircraft had a wing of variable incidence. The X-5's wing incidence could be changed in flight, whereas the P.1101's could only be changed on the ground. Two X-5s were built, and the first flight was at Edwards with Bell pilot Jean "Skip" Ziegler on June 20, 1951. The X-5 was the first aircraft to fly with a "swing wing." The photograph's multiple exposure illustrates this total wing movement nicely. (AFFTC.)

Here is another mishap saved by the forgiving nature of the dry lakebed's clay surface: the X-5 No. 1 lands with collapsed landing gear. The NACA used the X-5 from 1952 through most of 1955 to investigate variable-sweep wing flight characteristics. The aircraft was also used as a chase plane because of its ability to match the flight ranges of other aircraft. On October 14, 1953, air force pilot Maj. Raymond Popson was killed in a crash flying No. 2 X-5 after it failed to recover from a spin test. (DFRC.)

Sitting side by side on the ramp at the High-Speed Flight Station, the NACA's P2B-1S mother ship, Fertile Myrtle, and the agency's F-51D seem to be made for each other. The former P-51D was used for NACA pilot proficiency flights at Edwards from 1950 until 1958. The plane was previously stationed at the Langley Aeronautical Laboratory in Virginia. The U.S. Air Force had changed pursuit aircraft (P) to fighters (F) in the time the NACA acquired its Mustang, hence the F-51D designation. (DFRC.)

As this 1953 photograph demonstrates, one couldn't accuse the NACA of wasting government money on a surplus of hangars at Edwards. Many NACA projects were stored in the High-Speed Flight Station's crowded main hangar. Packed together that day were, clockwise from the left, three Skyrockets (two not visible in this photograph), an X-4, an ETF-51D, B-47D, a Skystreak, X-5, X-1, XF-92A, YRF-84F up front, and behind it, another Skystreak. (DFRC.)

Here is the same hangar a few years later. Behind the Gooney Bird at the doors are a couple of F-100s, a JF-102, an F-51 and a B-47. (DFRC.)

NACA test pilot Scott Crossfield walked away from this low-speed crash into the facility's main hangar in 1954. This F-100A was flown by the NACA to help determine why the early Super Sabres were killing pilots, including North American Aviation's chief test pilot, George Welch. The hot new air force fighter had directional-stability and roll-coupling problems. Research flights and some dicey but well-documented moments convinced North American Aviation (NAA) to increase the size of the vertical stabilizer and wingtips; that did the trick on subsequent production models. Crossfield met the hangar wall after an emergency dead stick landing and fast rollout that faded the brakes. (DFRC.)

In this 1956 photograph, fashion-conscious engineers Cliff Morris and Thomas Sisk discuss something at the Alpha-Beta vane on a Convair YF-102 Delta Dart on the NACA ramp. The YF-102 arrived at the High-Speed Flight Station in 1954 and made about 100 flights over the next four years. The YF-102 was a larger, fighter version of the XF-92 experimental aircraft, which first flew on June 9, 1948. The Delta Dart also differed with canopy and inlet changes. The YF-102 initially flew in October 1953, while production for the F-102 was slowly underway with the benefit of prototype test planes. Test flights with this version, the F-102A, began at Edwards in June 1955. (DFRC.)

Anticipated as a supersonic fighter, the F-102 was not a Mach buster until NACA engineer Richard Whitcomb's newly derived area-rule principle was applied to the design, lengthening the fuselage and slimming it at the wing roots, seen here on the JF-102A. The so-called wasp or coke-bottle waist was a game-changer in high-speed aerodynamic design and used on many subsequent supersonic aircraft. The JF-102A was flown by the NACA from 1956 to 1959. (DFRC.)

Standing next to the entry hatch of a Boeing B-47 Stratojet are NACA pilots Joe Walker (left) and Stan Butchart (right) talking to Stratojet crew chief Wilbur McClenaghan. Above them, technicians work on an air data probe meant to gather information while the jet was in flight. The NACA conducted a series of tests on aeroelasiticity of wings using the B-47, which was on loan from the U.S. Air Force. (DFRC.)

By the mid-1950s, after the tragic, fatal last flight of the X-2, it became obvious that conventional flight control surfaces were not enough at the dizzying altitudes now within reach of the aircraft at Edwards. Above 100,000 feet, aerodynamic controls needed to give way to small thrusters, like a spacecraft. Engineers at the NACA High-Speed Flight Station thought the X-1B could be modified with thrusters and used as a test bed for reaction controls. In preparation for flight tests, this contraption, known as the Iron Cross, was built to simulate the flight characteristics of the X-1B using reaction controls. Six thrusters using pressurized nitrogen gas provided control in pitch, roll, and yaw. In the above photograph, NACA pilot Stan Butchart imparts some roll to the left during a hop in 1956. Below, Butchart demonstrates for a sub-committee. (Both: DFRC.)

Here one of NASA's F-104s has been modified with a reaction control system utilizing small hydrogen peroxide thrusters in the nose and wing tips, the same kind that would appear on the U.S. Air Force's NF-104s in the early 1960s. The hydrogen peroxide passed over silver screens and decomposed into steam, seen here exhausting under pressure from a nozzle in the nose. (DFRC.)

A youthful Neil Armstrong poses next to a NASA F-104 chase plane. Armstrong began flying with the NACA at Edwards in 1955. During the next seven years there, until he left for the NASA astronaut program, he made over 900 flights in an impressive variety of prop, jet, and rocket planes. (DFRC.)

The North American F-100A made its maiden flight at Edwards on May 25, 1953. In 1954, there were an alarming number of flight incidents, and after a catastrophic accident over the desert due to inertial coupling, which killed NAA test pilot George Welch, the plane was grounded. Flight research by the NACA that year lead to increasing the vertical fin's surface by 27 percent. NAA adopted the larger fin, increased the wingspan, and the problem was fixed. Here is the NACA-modified plane compared to a standard F-100A. (DFRC.)

Following a nose gear collapse on landing in 1956, the Bell X-1E came to a slightly ignominious rest. The X-1E was the X-1 No. 2 with modifications, including an ejection seat and thinner wings to prolong its life in research, but by 1956, the 1940s rocket plane had little to offer compared to new aircraft of the day. (DFRC.)

JATOs helped shorten takeoff rolls, but here is a zero-roll, rocket-assisted takeoff of an F-100 from a truck bed. A U.S. Air Force newsreel described it at the time as a "130,000 pound kick in the pants" that propelled the Super Sabre from zero to 275 miles per hour in four seconds. The project was called ZELL, short for zero-length launch. This 1958 Cold War program was conceived to provide a way for fighters to take to the skies in the event that air base runways were destroyed or damaged by a surprise enemy attack. (AFFTC.)

Once again, the lakebed tells a graphic story of a landing that did not end as planned. NASA's F-107A is being towed away after a ground loop in 1959. The NACA took delivery of the first and third of three North American YF-107As after they were rejected for the F-105 as a new U.S. Air Force fighter. The first was a maintenance nuisance and was grounded after four flights. The other became a useful test bed during 1958–1959 for evaluating side-stick flight controls. The YF-107A made its first flight at Edwards on September 10, 1956, ending with a drag chute failure during rollout, followed by the nose gear collapsing after hitting a dip in the lakebed at a high speed. Below, a maintenance crew works on the first F-107A in the Dryden hangar. (Both: DFRC.)

Three

BRIDGING AIR AND SPACE

From the late 1950s until the mid-1970s, the ambitions of the flight test and research programs at Edwards were astonishing. Independent and joint flight test programs by the air force, navy and NACA/NASA developed rocket planes that flew to edge of space and wingless vehicles as prototypes for future spacecraft. Less exotic, but still revolutionary programs refined the way planes flew, increasing safety and efficiency. Finally, when NASA's space shuttle *Columbia* landed on Rogers Dry Lake after its first orbital flight, the gap between air and space operations at Edwards closed. Above, NASA pilot Milt Thompson sits in the cockpit of the M2-F2 wingless lifting body, framed by the reflection of the craft's B-52 mother ship. (DFRC.)

Standing on a wet ramp are three pilots expected to fly the X-15. They are, from left to right, Neil Armstrong (NASA), Iven Kincheloe (U.S. Air Force), and Robert White (U.S. Air Force). Kincheloe was then the fastest- and highest-flying man alive, but before he could join the X-15 program, he was killed during an ejection from an F-104. (AFFTC.)

Test pilot Scott Crossfield left the NACA to fly for North American Aviation, becoming the first pilot on the X-15. He experienced a problem on one of the very first flights of the new rocket plane. He could not dump all the fuel before landing, and shortly after touchdown on Rosamond Dry Lake, the airplane's back broke. Firemen worked on the vehicle wearing the proper protection from the plane's volatile and caustic soup of fuels and oxidizers. This X-15 was rebuilt by NAA and flown again. (DFRC.)

This is the first class of X-15 pilots. Pictured from left to right are Forrest Petersen (U.S. Navy), Neil Armstrong (NASA), Robert Rushworth (U.S. Air Force), John "Jack" McKay (NASA), Robert White (U.S. Air Force), and Joe Walker (NASA). Below, the group is in a lighter mood. (Both: DFRC.)

In this 1959 photograph, six of the Mercury Seven astronauts visit the Flight Research Center. The man seated, X-15 pilot Joe Walker, shows them the world's first space plane. They are, clockwise from left to right, Scott Carpenter, Gordon Cooper, Gus Grissom, John Glenn, Alan Shepard, and Wally Schirra. It's easy to imagine Walker's pride and the other pilots' interest in the new machine. (DFRC.)

On a visit a couple years after the previous photograph, NASA's father of the moon program, Wernher von Braun, checks out the X-15. Von Braun was a pilot and could well appreciate the significance of an airplane that would literally fly into space and back to Earth. (DFRC.)

The top photograph was taken during an X-15 preflight briefing. Briefings allowed flight crews, engineers, X-15 operations director, ground controller, and others another chance to compare notes and finalize flight plans. Many of the same people would meet again in the Control Room. Pictured below is the NASA X-15 control room during a flight in 1961. Seated second from the left is X-15 pilot Jack McKay. The X-15's flight path covered three states and it took the B-52 mother ship an hour and a half simply to reach the launch point. By 1959, telemetry made it possible to watch the aircraft's systems in real time. The X-15 control room concept was adopted almost entirely by the Mercury program and then by the Gemini and Apollo programs. (Above: AFFTC; below: DFRC.)

Above is a snapshot of X-15 close out process. The pilot is in the cockpit waving as crew members continue to make last minute checks right up until they close the canopy. The air conditioning pack that sits on the top of the air stairs is still hooked up to White and will stay as such until the B-52 powers up. (AFFTC.)

This is an X-15 dropping away from the NB-52B just after release. In order to accommodate the X-15, the bomber had its flaps permanently locked in the retracted position. This made for very long take-off rolls, especially when carrying a payload like the X-15. Eight of the 12 men who flew the X-15 earned astronaut wings for having reached space in the vehicle. (DFRC.)

Here is an X-15 shortly after a landing. The Piasecki H-21 "Flying Banana" helicopter in the background was always present at landings in case of an emergency. Notice the somewhat informal approach to high risk and high tech research flying, epitomized by the casual dress and pose of the three men standing around the open cockpit, with the pilot still inside. (AFFTC.)

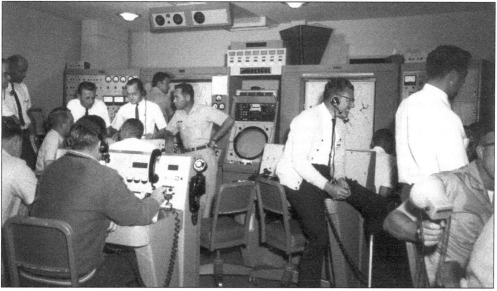

This photograph was taken in a control room for an X-15 flight in 1966. William "Pete" Knight, standing center in the image wearing his air force uniform, was the voice of the control room in all communications with the X-15 pilot on this flight. Knight was then an X-15 pilot himself. This tradition, having a pilot who had flown the X-15 as the voice of "NASA One," carried over to the NASA rocket programs, in which case it was an astronaut who spoke from the control room.

Royal Air Force squadron leader Harry Archer and U.S. Air Force major Jack Allavie strike a pose in front of the NB-52B mother ship. Prelaunch preparations are underway on the X-15 seen over Archer's shoulder. (AFFTC.)

Pete Knight is lowering himself into the cockpit of the X-15A-2. This X-15 had a white ablative coating meant to protect the aircraft while conducting flights at its highest speeds. The ship also sported external fuel tanks, boosting the engine run and giving the plane a higher Mach number. On October 3, 1967, Knight reached the record speed of 4,520 miles per hour (Mach 6.7). The aircraft suffered such severe burns that even though it was repaired, it never flew again. (AFFTC.)

Out of the 20 X-15 flights in 1966, four of them, like the one pictured above, ended with unscheduled landings at one of the several dry lakes below the planned flight path but outside of Edwards. Emergency planning throughout the X-15 program provided for rescue personnel, fire trucks (in a C-130), and other support aircraft that could immediately render assistance in these remote locations. Thanks to the exceptional flying skills of the X-15 pilots, the strength of airframes, and quick rescues, emergency landings ended safely, even in the case of a landing accident. Afterward, the plane's tail was dismantled and the aircraft was trucked back to Edwards, with the occasional pit stop along the way. (Both: DFRC.)

In 1961, United Artists produced a feature film about the X-15 called simply *X-15*. It was directed by Richard Donner and starred a young Charles Bronson as an intrepid test pilot. NASA X-15 pilot Milt Thompson was the film's technical advisor, and he recalled that at one point an actor-pilot had no problem wearing the pressure suit, climbing into an X-15 cockpit, and closing the helmet visor—something even experienced pilots find frightfully claustrophobic. However, when the plane's canopy was lowered and latched, he panicked and pounded on the windows with his fists. The scene was cut. The top photograph shows how the X-15 hangar was composed for the movie; below is the Dryden hangar on a real workday. (Both: DFRC.)

Here the second group of X-15 pilots poses for a formal picture. They are, from left to right, Joe Engle (U.S. Air Force), Robert "Bob" Rushworth (U.S. Air Force), John "Jack" McKay (NASA), William "Pete" Knight (U.S. Air Force), Milton "Milt" Thompson (NASA), and William "Bill" Dana (NASA). Below, a coworker in the project office added cartoon bubbles to an informal portrait. (Both: DFRC.)

This is what happens when an F-104 "augers-in" at high speed. In 1962, NASA pilot Milt Thompson was simulating X-15 approaches in a JF-104A at high altitude and tried to lower the flaps. One flap actuator failed, setting up rolls that became uncontrollable. Thompson ejected. The plane exploded on impact, while observers on the ground failed see the Thompson's descent with the parachute. With only news of the crash and no word about the well-liked pilot, gloom quickly spread at NASA Dryden. Meanwhile, Thompson landed safely, walked to a nearby road, and waited to hitch a ride to the crash site. Soon a NASA car approached, and inside was the chief of flight operations. Thompson flagged it down, and they headed back to Dryden. (DFRC.)

This is a photograph of Chuck Yeager in a Lockheed NF-104G on December 4, 1963. The U.S. Air Force had Lockheed permanently modify three F-104As (hence the "N" prefix) for the purpose of zoom climbs so that pilots could reach 120,000 feet. The aircraft had a Rocketdyne AR2-3 rocket motor in the tail to push the aircraft the last leg of the climb, in the region where the air was so thin the jet engine would die. Each jet also had reaction control thrusters in the wingtips and the nose to control the aircraft in the thin air at the peak altitude. Yeager destroyed the third NF-104A when he had to bail out during a flight on December 10, 1963. At right is a close-up of the NF-104A rocket motor. (Both: AFFTC.)

Pictured above, two remarkable aircraft stand on display at Edwards in 1963 with men from both companies standing for review. On the left is the Convair B-58 Hustler, a Mach 2 bomber, and on the right is the DeHavilland Comet 2C. The Comet was the first jet to carry passengers in the west, but its life as an airliner was brief, being the first to suffer from what was then the unknown hazard of metal fatigue. The one in this photograph is a redesigned airframe, evident by the circular windows. It was the nearly square windows on the first DH.1 Comet that led to metal fatigue because of repeated pressurization and depressurization. (AFFTC.)

The B-58 originally had ejection seats for its three crew members, but concern about the survivability of Mach 2 ejections at high altitudes led to the development of Stanley Aircraft Corporation ejection capsules. This photographic sequence shows the testing of a capsule at Edwards. The tests were done while the Hustler was performing a high-speed taxi. The capsules were retrofitted into the bombers beginning in late 1962. (AFFTC.)

Air force pilots Joe Jordan and Harry Brown squat down and pose in front of the escape pod of the General Dynamics F-111, which saved their lives on January 2, 1968. Like the XB-70 and the B-58, and unlike most other aircraft, the F-111 had a pod in which the crew left the stricken aircraft. In the F-111's case, the pod took both crew members together. In the case of the other aircraft mentioned above, a single pod took each crew member out individually and sealed him from the atmosphere until he was down. The assumption was that an ejection at speeds of Mach 2 or above without such protection would kill the occupant. It certainly worked for Jordan and Brown. The F-111 first flew in December 1964, with production models entering service in 1967. An F-111A was delivered to Dryden in 1967 for a NASA/U.S. Air Force/General Dynamics program addressing the problem of engine compressor stalls and surges on the early F-111s. The research lead to inlet changes that resolved the issues. Dryden continued to engage an F-111 in various flight research programs during the 1970s and 1980s. (AFFTC.)

After the downing of Francis Gary Powers during an over flight of the Soviet Union in a CIA-operated Lockheed U-2 spy plane, the U.S. government presented a cover story to try and defuse the event. The government argued that the U-2 was merely a weather plane that had strayed off course. To bolster the story, the government had at least one U-2 brought to the Flight Research Center, adorned it with NACA markings, and then released pictures to the public. This photograph, taken on May 6, 1960, is of the U-2 on the back ramp of the Flight Research Center on May 6, 1960. The ruse did not work. Ironically, the U-2s did carry NACA instrumentation on occasion to study weather. (DFRC.)

A black Lockheed U-2 flies almost directly over the taxiway leading from NASA to the Main Base and its main runway. To the left of the taxiway are contractors' hangars, giving the area the name "contractors' way." It is here that firms such as North American Aviation and Douglas Aircraft Company maintained support staff and equipment while a particular aircraft of theirs was being demonstrated. On the ramp is a NAA XB-70 bomber. (AFFTC.)

Taken from the opposite direction as the previous image, this picture shows two Lockheed U-2s. The hangar in the bottom right is unusual. Notice that it has two notches above the sliding main doors—to accommodate the two vertical stabilizers of the XB-70 so the plane can be towed into the hangar. There are identical notches on the other end of the hangar so the bomber can be towed directly out. (AFFTC.)

Fitzhugh "Fitz" Fulton is in the cockpit of a Convair B-58 Hustler. Fulton performed much of the testing on the B-58 at Edwards, and after a long air force career, he came to NASA, where he flew the B-52 mother ship, XB-70, and many other aircraft. Fulton served in World War II and flew numerous missions in C-54s into Berlin during the Berlin Airlift at the start of the Cold War. (AFFTC.)

The North American Aviation XB-70 Valkyrie was an experimental supersonic bomber. NAA built two airframes for the U.S. Air Force, but by the time they were delivered, the air force had decided against the design. After the air force tested the planes, NASA opted to use the faster of the two for high-speed research, but before that could happen, it was lost in an accident in 1966. The agency used the second airframe instead. The above photograph looks down on one on the ramp. Below, the XB-70 is being chased by a Convair B-58 Hustler. While other aircraft were also used to fly chase on the XB-70, when the Valkyrie flew Mach 2 and above, the only aircraft that could keep up for any length of time was the B-58. (Both: AFFTC.)

Pictured at right are NASA XB-70 pilots Don Mallick and Fitz Fulton in 1968. What is apparent from this angle is that the fuselage rises gradually from the wing until, by the wing's forwardmost point, the fuselage is completely above the wing. NAA spent thousands of hours conducting wind tunnel research developing compression lift, which used the shock wave created by the forward section of the aircraft to develop lift that the wing captured, making flight at supersonic speeds more efficient than it otherwise would be. (DFRC.)

The aft end of the tall Valkyrie shows its six GE YJ93 jet engines. Each engine produced a bit less than a maximum of 30,000 pounds of thrust. (AFFTC.)

The NACA acquired two of the only four built Douglas F5D-1 Skylancers in the late 1950s and based them at Moffet Field. They were moved to NASA Dryden in 1961 and used at Edwards to fly simulated landing approaches for the Dyna-Soar X-20A spaceplane in development at the time. Dyna-Soar was a U.S.Air Force/Boeing program that was to use a small, shuttle-like spacecraft boosted into orbit atop a Titan III rocket. The Skylancer was chosen for this project because its wing planform was similar to the X-20A. NASA Dryden pilot Neil Armstrong developed a training exercise that would duplicate a landing approach used by the X-20A during an aborted launch. The landing maneuver was based upon some basic aerobatics and became very popular with the pilots at Edwards. Dyna-Soar was cancelled in 1963. (DFRC.)

With an NACA/NASA strip on the tail, a NASA "meatball," and sporting flourishes elsewhere, this Douglas Skytrain seems a cross between an airliner and test ship. In some ways it was, as one of three C-47/R4Ds used by the NACA and NASA from 1952 to 1984. Pictured here landing during a flight in 1964, this plane was a workhorse. It was used to transport equipment and people to locations outside of Edwards, sometimes to other dry lakes in support of the X-15 program, and as the tow plane for 77 flights of the original lifting body, the M2-F1. (DFRC.)

Here is another example of the wonderful ironies at Edwards in the early 1960s. In this 1962 image is a skinny motorcycle, the spindly Paresev paraglider, and an old Stearman biplane (used to tow the Paresev aloft). It doesn't immediately impress one with a vision of the space age, but it's the future cobbled together with support from the past. The Francis Rogallo Wing-inspired Paresev was built at NASA Dryden to begin the development of flexible, inflatable wings for Gemini spacecraft to allow for a landing, rather than splashdown. Most of the people in the photograph also helped develop and fly the first lifting bodies, including pilot Milt Thompson, who was also flying to the edge of space in the X-15 during this period. On the motorcycle is Walter "Whitey" Whiteside, in the Paresev 1-A is Thompson, and standing are, from left to right, Frank Fedor, Richard Klein, Victor Horton, Tom Kelly Jr., Fred Harris (owner of the Stearman), John Orahood, and Gary Layton. The concept was tested with several wing configurations, but the final, inflatable wing version was very unstable, and the program was cancelled. (DFRC.)

The space age looms over the jet age. NASA's Lunar Landing Research Vehicle (LLRV) hovers about 1,500 feet above two cold war icons, the B-47 and B-58. The LLRV, sometimes called "the Flying Bedstead," was developed to provide an in-flight simulator to train Apollo astronauts how to land on the moon. Using analog computers, a center-mounted, gimballed jet engine, and hydrogen-peroxide thrusters, the LLRV effectively simulated flight conditions under the moon's gravity and the vacuum of space. (DFRC.)

NASA pilot Joe Walker was the first to fly the LLRV. The above photograph shows Walker after a flight. In 1964, Pres. Lyndon Johnson visited Edwards, and the base rolled out most of its major projects for him to review. NASA put the X-15 and LLRV on display. Below, Walker leans in to show Johnson how the LLRV controls work while Flight Research Center director Paul Bikle looks on. (Both: DFRC.)

One of the great stories at NASA Dryden is the origin of the wingless lifting body aircraft. Above, Dryden engineer Dale R. Reed holds the M2-F1 lifting body model he crafted with balsa and tissue in 1962 to make the first flight tests of the blunt-nose, half-cone design that NACA researchers had proposed for spacecraft in the 1950s. The idea for a wingless reentry vehicle looked good on paper, but both NASA and U.S. Air Force space program leadership thought it too risky, maybe even ridiculous. Reed proved them wrong when his tiny models made stable, successful flights. Home movies of the flights convinced Dryden management to green light a test program using a full-scale, piloted version, seen behind Reed in this photograph. (DFRC.)

Here, the unpowered M2-F1 "flying bathtub" is being towed to a release altitude of 12,000 feet. The nose-high attitude allowed the pilot to keep the R4D tow plane in view. After wind tunnel testing and 48 tows to an altitude of 20 feet behind a hot rod Pontiac racing across the dry lake, the first flight was on a calm August 13, 1963. Nearly 60 years since the birth of aviation, this flight was like nothing before. With a descent rate of 3,600 feet per minute, test pilot Milt Thompson did not have much time to get a feel for the strange plane. He made a perfect landing. Below are more models with, from left to right, engineers Jim Love, Gene Matranga, Dale Reed, and pilot Milt Thompson in 1963. (Both: DFRC.)

Surrounding air force pilot Chuck Yeager in the cockpit are NASA pilots, from left to right, Milt Thompson, Bruce Peterson, and Don Mallick. All flew the M2-F1. Other pilots who had time in the aircraft were NASA pilots Fred Haise and Bill Dana and air force pilots Capt. Jerry Gentry, Maj. James Wood, Capt. Joe Engle, and Maj. Donald Sorlie. Yeager, who was in command of the Aerospace Research Pilots School at Edwards at the time, made five flights in the lifting body. He enjoyed flying it and requested to do a barrel roll on his last flight. The project engineers feared the fragile tail might break up, and he was denied permission. A year later, the little craft endured a couple of accidental rolls, the last one pranging the airplane enough to end the flight program. (DFRC.)

With the success of the M2-F1, NASA pushed ahead with new lifting body programs, this time partnering with the Air Force Flight Test Center and major aircraft contractors. The Northrop M2-F2 was the first of the so-called "heavies." No more aero tows: the new aircraft were carried to altitude X-15-style, via B-52. Flying it as a glider, Milt Thompson made the first flight, a July 1966 jaunt lasting four minutes from a launch at 45,000 feet. It landed at 164 knots, followed by a mile-and-a-half rollout. Below, with a NASA F-104 chase plane for company, the lifting body is just about to land, the gear deployed moments before touchdown. (Both: DFRC.)

NASA pilot Bruce Peterson enjoys the moment before a flight in the M2-F2 in 1966. On a flight months later, he endured a spectacular crash landing; the crumpled remains of the vehicle are seen below. During this flight, Petersen sought to avoid a rescue helicopter that he felt was in his landing path. He extended the landing gear at the last moment—which all lifting body pilots did to avoid any unnecessary drag—and the gear failed to extend entirely before touchdown. Though Petersen survived the accident, he lost one eye. The M2-F2 was actually rebuilt, this time with a third vertical stabilizer for greater lateral stability, and went on to perform many more flights. A film clip of the crash was used in the title sequence of the 1960s television show *The Six Million Dollar Man*. (Both: DFRC.)

The M2-F3 was a rebuilt, rejiggered M2-F2, complete with an additional vertical fin that helped alleviate the control problems of the F2. It was now considered very controllable and pleasant to fly. Twenty-seven flights were made from June 1970 to December 1972. The rocket plane was flown to Mach 1.61. Continuing a line of research with reaction-control systems developed in the F-104 and X-15, the M2-F3 tested a rocket control system that worked very well. When the program ended, its engineers felt their technical reports would help in the design of future spacecraft. In the photograph below, the ever-popular NASA pilot Bill Dana's name is temporarily stenciled on the fin. (Both: DFRC.)

The Northrop HL-10 was yet another take on wingless design and had a body shaped almost like an inverted airfoil. The HL-10 had serious control problems at first—the maiden flight with Bruce Peterson lasted a hair-raising 189 seconds from 45,000 feet, with Peterson keeping the speed higher than planned to maintain control. The problems were eventually resolved, and the HL-10 was regarded as relatively easy to fly. Pilots came to like it so much they jokingly fought over who would fly it next, as the photograph below suggests with, clockwise from left, project pilots Bill Dana, John Manke, Pete Hoag, and Jerry Gentry. The flight program lasted from December 1966 until July 1970. (Both: DFRC.)

The HL-10 is shown making its typical steep descent for landing on Rogers Dry Lake. The aircraft will in fact land on the marked runway, located in the lower right to upper left of the image. North Base is visible on the edge of the lakebed. (DFRC.)

This iconic photograph shows NASA pilot Bill Dana after landing the HL-10 lifting body on Rogers Dry Lake. The crew of the B-52 mother ship shows their respect to the research vehicle crew with a low pass above them before landing on Edwards's main runway. (DFRC.)

Some cast members of the late-1960s television series *Star Trek* check out the futuristic lifting bodies during a visit Dryden. Seen here next to the HL-10 are James Doohan, the actor who played "Scotty" (second from left); series creator Gene Roddenberry (fifth from left); and DeForest Kelley, the actor who portrayed "Bones" (third from right). (AFFTC.)

117

Three approaches to wingless flight are pictured in 1969. On the left, the Martin Aircraft Company X-24A was based upon the Martin SV-5 concept. The U.S. Air Force conducted three tests of the SV-5D, a small, unpiloted craft with an ablative heat shield, to speeds of nearly 15,000 miles per hour using Atlas rocket boosters in 1966–1967. Those tests, combined with the piloted X-24A flights, demonstrated successful maneuvering flight through nearly the complete speed range of orbital reentry from Mach 24 to landing. In less than nine years, the lifting body went from one man's balsa-and-tissue glider to a viable spacecraft design. (DFRC.)

Maj. Cecil Powell poses proudly after a powered flight in the X-24A in 1971. Powell and Maj. Gerald "Jerry" Gentry were the U.S. Air Force pilots on the flight program, while John Manke flew the chubby rocket plane for NASA. The pilots prepared for each eight-minute research flight with about 20 hours on a ground simulator, plus flying another 60 or so X-24A landing profiles in an F-104. (DFRC.)

In 1970, NASA and the U.S. Air Force partnered on a new lifting body project using the X-24A structure surrounded by a new shell. Martin Marietta Corporation finished the modifications in 1972, giving birth to the most futuristic-looking lifting body, the X-24B. It now had a flat bottom and was 14.5 feet longer and 10 feet wider. The X-24B was expected to have "slap-down" landings similar to the X-15. To make sure that the structure and nose gear would hold up during high loads, a number of slap-down tests were made at Dryden. During tests, the nose was dropped while the structure pivoted on the secured main gear. This aerial photograph with an F-104 chase plane serves as a reminder of how steep the descents could be. (Both: DFRC.)

With the gear still up, here is the sleek X-24B just before a lakebed landing. The wedge-like aircraft had the highest landing lift-to-drag ratio of the lifting bodies, 4.5, which is comparable to the space shuttle. Air force and NASA pilots gave the X-24B high marks for its handling qualities, some comparing it to the T-38 and F-104 (seen flying chase in the photograph below). On two separate flights in August 1975, pilots John Manke and Mike Love made spot landings on the concrete runway at Edwards, one of which can be seen in the photograph below. They proved that safe and accurate landings with these kinds of aircraft are possible on conventional runways. The last flight was on November 26, 1975, marking the end of an era at Edwards. (Both: DFRC.)

In 1976, an Aero Spacelines Super Guppy—a blimp-like, 1957-era Boeing 377 modified to ferry Apollo spacecraft boosters—was used to transport the now venerable X-24B and HL-10 lifting bodies to the U.S. Air Force Museum in Ohio. Lessons learned from the lifting body projects influenced the space shuttle development, but over 40 years after the first lifting body flight, there was yet to be a space-rated version of this visionary design. The HL-10 was eventually returned to NASA Dryden and is now mounted on a pole outside of the center's main entrance. (DFRC.)

No, this is not an F-15 with experimental landing gear. It is a 3/8-scale F-15, one of three built by McDonnell Douglas Aircraft Company and used as remotely piloted research vehicles (RPRVs) to investigate the stall and spin characteristics of the F-15. Not as exotic as the lifting body projects of the early 1970s, it was typical of the many lower-profile programs at Edwards. The research program was based at NASA Dryden. The F-15 RPRVs were unpowered and flown as gliders after a trip to 45,000 feet under the wing of NASA's B-52 mother ship. Flights began in October 1973. Snatched in mid-air by helicopter during the early flights, the F-15 RPRVs were later flown to lakebed landings from a cockpit in the bowels of NASA Dryden, complete with a TV monitor providing an in-flight view. (DFRC.)

Vortex studies were not particularly glamorous in the realm of flight research, but they were at times visually stunning. Big, heavy aircraft such as this Boeing 747 generate little tornadoes trailing from the wingtips. NASA wanted to know more about these potentially dangerous wingtip vortices and their effect upon other aircraft. Tests using a Boeing 727 began in 1973 and a year later continued with this 747 that NASA bought from American Airlines. Smoke generators on the wings helped visualize wake turbulence. A Learjet and T-37 were then flown into the wake. It was found that vortices could completely roll either one of the smaller planes, even while flying miles behind the jumbo jet. This 747 was modified to transport space shuttles. (DFRC.)

Typical of flight research trends beginning in the early 1970s, an existing aircraft was modified rather than built from the ground up for the purpose of testing a new concept. In this case, a navy TF-8A Crusader was fitted with a new "supercritical wing." The sleek wing had an airfoil that was flatter on top than conventional wings to reduce the drag-inducing affects of a shock wave at speeds near Mach 1. The design was the brainchild of NASA aerodynamicist Dr. Richard Whitcomb, and the concept was proven to be correct with the F-8 SCW. The F-8 SCW did not have flaps or the variable-incidence wing of the original F-8, so the takeoff and landing speeds were higher than those of the Crusader. During another Dryden project using a Crusader, Dryden pilot Gary Krier made the first flight of an aircraft using only electronically dependant flight controls in May 1972. Superficially, the plane looked like a typical F-8C, but inside it was a different animal—its digital fly-by-wire controls paved the way for such systems in future civil and military aircraft. (DFRC.)

In 1977, NASA began atmospheric flight testing with the new space shuttle. Bringing the mother ship tradition into the space age, a Boeing 747 airliner was modified to carry the shuttle on its back and was later used to ferry the shuttles across the country. After five "captive-carry" flights, the shuttle made five glide flights from altitudes of 19,000 to 26,000 feet. The last landing resulted in a wild-looking pilot-induced oscillation (PIO) just before settling on the runway. The PIO led to more NASA flight research that delayed the shuttle program for several years but ultimately fixed the problem using other NASA aircraft. In these photographs, the shuttle is seen with and without the rocket engine tailcone. (DFRC.)

Edwards initially gained notoriety as the home of rugged test pilots and exotic aircraft. But with the shuttle glide flights, like the one seen below, its perception changed with the general public. In the top photograph, members of the 1960s *Star Trek* television show pose in front of the shuttle *Enterprise* in 1976. Pictured are, from left to right, NASA administrator Dr. James C. Fletcher, DeForest Kelley, George Takei, James Doohan, Nichelle Nichols, Leonard Nimoy, *Star Trek* series creator Gene Roddenberry, NASA deputy administrator George Low, and Walter Koenig. The television starship may have taken its name from a distinguished line of U.S. Navy vessels, but this first space shuttle clearly got its moniker from the fictional spaceship. When the shuttle orbiters started flying in 1981, Edwards became "the place where the space shuttles land." (Both: DFRC.)

Visit us at
arcadiapublishing.com